When Children Worked

by Robert Morales

HOUGHTON MIFFLIN BOSTON

What if you didn't go to school or outside
to play in the morning? What if you went to work
instead? That is what life was like for approximately
two million children less than 100 years ago.

Children worked in coal mines, on farms, and in factories. Some factory jobs started at 6:00 A.M., and the children worked until 8:00 P.M. with only 30 minutes for lunch.

In the coal mines, a nine-year-old boy might work for 10 hours each day and be paid around 60 cents. The work was extremely hard, and sometimes it was dangerous.

In the late 1800s, industry in America boomed. Factories were built to manufacture all kinds of things, but the pay for adults was very low. Children worked to help support their families. A factory owner might hire children because they were paid even less than adults. Also, children's small hands were able to reach into places where adults' hands couldn't.

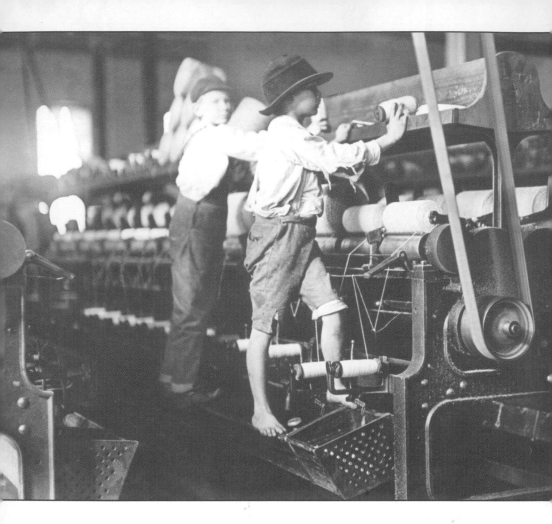

In a factory where cloth is made, called a textile mill, the children were sometimes injured by the machines. Beginning in the late 1840s, states began to pass laws stating that children could not work in these places. However, the number of working children kept growing until 1910.

Then some factories began using an assembly line to make things. On an assembly line, the worker stands in one place. The thing being made moves past the line of workers. Each worker adds one part to the item.

Assembly lines lowered the cost of making products. Eventually, factory workers were paid more, and parents started to send children to school, not to work. In 1938, a law was passed forbidding business owners to employ children under the age of 14.

Wouldn't you rather go to school?